Deposition Prep

A book to help you prepare for your deposition.

A book to help you understand the rules and reasons behind the deposition.

Table of Contents

DISCLAIMERS:

- This book is not intended to give legal advice but to provide you with practical information about depositions.
- Reading this book does not create an attorney-client relationship.
- Please be sure to speak with an attorney in your area.
- I am licensed to practice law only in the state of Arizona.
- Although I may reference other states, my only experience is with Arizona Courts. But much of what is written in this book is applicable in all states. Just be sure to check your state's rules, procedures and statutes.
- Remember, laws and rules change daily. Any laws or definitions listed in this book could change the next day. The purpose of the book is not to provide or explain the laws, but only to help guide you through the process.
- The laws that are listed should be verified by each reader at the time of reading and prior to your deposition.
- Should you have any questions, you should seek input from an attorney in your area.

ABOUT ME

I have been practicing law since 2000. In 2018, I decided to focus my practice on preparing other attorneys' clients for hearings, depositions, custody evaluation, vocational evaluations and the like, though my business Strategic Legal Services. I've found that being prepared not only assists the parties to more effectively present the facts necessary to help their case, but also knowing what to expect helps to keep them calmer during the process. If you have any questions about my business, please visit the website www.StrategicLegalServicesAZ.com.

After writing the custody evaluation prep book, I realized that I could help self-represented litigants prepare for their divorce case just as I helped prepare parties for custody evaluations.

In 2012 I created a company called ProperComm. We edit emails and text messages between high conflict families. ProperComm is ordered by courts nationwide and is free for victims of domestic violence if ordered that way by the court. Please visit our website www.ProperComm.com. I received a patent for the process we use in ProperComm to edit messages. Please visit our website.

My objective is not to provide legal advice, but to help you through your deposition.

Introduction

If you are reading this book, you are likely involved, some way, in a litigation; and you are likely going to be deposed and you need to prepare to ensure you present your best self and your best information. This book will provide necessary information to help you understand what to expect, how to testify and how to react in certain situations that may arise and how to present your best self.

Although there are Federal Rules for depositions, each state has its own individual rules. Furthermore, the rules may be different depending on the type of case. For instance, Civil Rules may be different from Criminal Rules; and although Family Law is a type of Civil Law, those rules may be altogether different. Furthermore, Bankruptcy and Tax Court are federal courts and must follow Federal Rules. It is important to know the rules in your jurisdiction. The importance and reasons for knowing the rules will be set forth more fully below.

The more you know, the more comfortable you are. The more comfortable you are, the better the experience will be. When you know what to expect, and you eliminate the element of surprise, you are able to respond more peacefully, more professionally, and less emotionally.

Frequently asked questions

1. What is a deposition?

    A deposition is a witnesses sworn out of court testimony.
    (www.law.cornell.edu)

    Depositions are a form of discovery. Discovery is used by
    attorneys and litigants to gather information and
    evidence to help prove their cases. Taking a party's
    deposition is one way for attorneys to obtain out of
    court, sworn testimony.

    When someone takes your deposition, you will be sworn
    in, just like you would be sworn in at court and you will
    be required to tell the truth while answering questions.

2. Who can depose a person?

    Typically, attorneys do the deposing. However, if a party
    is representing herself, she may be permitted to depose
    the other party or necessary witnesses.

3. Do I have to attend a deposition?

    Probably. If you have been properly subpoenaed or
    noticed, you will likely be required to appear at a
    deposition and give sworn testimony. Parties to the
    litigation typically agree to appear and do not always
    require a subpoena. However, you may receive a Notice
    to Appear or an Order to Appear or a Subpoena to
    Appear which should have the time, date and address
    where you are to appear listed.

If you are not a party to the litigation, you may or may not be required to attend the deposition. If you are not volunteering to be deposed, or if one of the parties opposes you being deposed, the party requesting the deposition will likely be required to obtain a court order allowing the deposition to take place. If they receive the court order, and you did not object, you will be required to attend and they will likely serve a subpoena upon you.

However, the subpoena itself should provide information on how you can object to the subpoena.

4. What if I refuse to attend the deposition?

When you are subpoenaed for a deposition, the subpoena should include information about how you can object to it and the basis for objections.

Reasons to object (Federal Rules of Civil Procedure, Rule 45):
- Late notice
- Undue burden
- Requires a person to comply by attending a deposition beyond the geographical limit specified in Rule 45 (c)[1].

If you are a party to the litigation, and you were properly subpoenaed[2] you may be held in contempt if you do not appear and the court did not grant your objection to appearing.

---

[1] Federal Rule permit require compliance at 100-mile radius.
[2] Parties to litigations often agree to appear and work with the deposing attorney to ensure a deposition time, date, and location that is convenient for all.

5. Can I bring my spouse/mom/girlfriend/boyfriend with me?

    You will need to check the rules in your jurisdiction. However, you may be permitted to bring someone with you to the deposition unless a protective order has been filed and granted[3].

    If it is a family law case and you are bringing a new significant other, that person may be precluded for good cause.

6. Do I have to answer every question?

    It depends on the question.
    - You are not required to testify against yourself. Therefore, if you are being asked about a crime, you will want to speak with your attorney about pleading the Fifth Amendment. That means that you are not willing to incriminate yourself by stating that you have committed a crime. However, it is important to understand that in a civil court, that can be used against you.
        - Example: Did you hit your wife?

            If you did hit your wife, and you answer honestly, the deposition statement/testimony can be used against you in a criminal case. So, you may want to plead the Fifth.

---

[3] Federal Rules of Civil Procedure, Rule 26(c)5.

- You are not required to divulge attorney client privilege information.
    - Example: What did your attorney tell you?

        Your attorney should object to ensure you do not disclose any attorney client privileged information.

- You may not be permitted to divulge trade secrets.
    - Example: What are the ingredients in the secret sauce.

        Your attorney would likely stop you from answering that question.

- You may not be required to testify against your spouse due to the spousal communication privilege also known as marital privilege.
    - Example: Did your wife tell you that she was going to embezzle money from her employer?

        Your attorney or your spouse's attorney should stop you from disclosing privileged information.

7. Is the person taking the deposition allowed to be mean?

    Being "mean" is subjective. Attorneys are required to be professional. If an attorney is unprofessional during a deposition, that may be cause to let the attorney know you believe you are being harassed, oppressed or embarrassed and that you want them to stop immediately. The federal rules, and likely the rules in your jurisdiction, may permit a deposition to be ended if certain requirements are met, i.e. you are being harassed, unnecessarily embarrassed, etc.

Be sure to know the rules in your jurisdiction. Furthermore, be sure to warn the attorney prior to just stopping the deposition. The courts want discovery to be completed, but they also want to protect the parties during the discovery process. Therefore, you would want to give the questioning attorney a warning before ending the deposition.

It is also important to understand that there may be rules you must follow if you do stop the deposition. For instance, you may need to file a Motion or a Notice to the Court within a certain time period. If you do not follow the rules, you may be sanctioned and the attorney may have another opportunity to depose you. Furthermore, even if you do follow all the rules, the other attorney may be permitted time to question you more, but the subject matter may be limited.

Costs of Deposition

There are several costs associated with having your deposition taken or taking someone else's deposition.

1. <u>Court Reporter Fees</u>: The court reporter will have fees for showing up and taking the deposition. Those fees are separate from all other fees.

2. <u>Videographer</u>: If you have the deposition video recorded, you may have someone other than the Court Reporter controlling that. That will likely be a separate cost.

3. <u>Transcription Costs:</u> Ordering the transcript will be a separate expense. The cost will vary depending on the length of the deposition.

4. <u>Expedited Costs:</u> If you want to get the deposition transcribed faster than the court reporter's normal turn-around time, you will likely be required to pay a significant amount more.

5. <u>Expert Fees:</u> If you decide to depose an expert, you should understand it can be quite expensive. You will likely be required to pay their hourly fees for reviewing their notes, travel, and deposition testimony. You will also likely be required to pay it prior to their appearance.

6. <u>Attorney Fees:</u> If you have an attorney, you will likely be required to pay for their time at the deposition and also their time to prepare for the deposition. If your attorney will be deposing someone, it will likely take them several hours to prepare questions.

7. <u>Opposing Party's Attorney Fees:</u> The court can require you to pay attorney fees in some cases. If the court does decide you should pay the opposing parties' attorney fees, you may be stuck with those costs too.

Rules of Depositions

The rules of deposition should be listed in your court rules. As stated above, you should be familiar with the rules in your jurisdiction. I recommend printing them and taking them into the deposition with you if you are not represented.

There are some basic rules, listed below, that are found throughout most jurisdictions.

Attendance

You should receive a notice or a subpoena requiring you to attend your deposition. That notice or subpoena should be set our far enough in time to allow you to make plans for child care, request time off from work, arrange for transportation and the like.

The subpoena should provide you with the date, time, and location of the deposition and let you know what, if anything you are required to bring to the deposition.

The subpoena should state if the deposition will be video recorded.

The subpoena should also state the circumstances which would permit you to object and the number of days you have to do so.

Be sure to read each page of the subpoena carefully.

Swearing In

You will be sworn in and you will be required to tell the truth, just like you would in trial.

After you are sworn in, you will be asked questions and you will be required to answer the question. If you are not honest during your deposition, it can be used against you.

Video Deposition vs Court Reporter vs Online Video Deposition

It is important to know if your deposition will be video recorded. If it is, you may want to dress differently and ensure you are presentable for court, not just a deposition. Dressing for a video deposition will be explained below. It will be up to the deposing attorney to determine if the deposition will be video recorded.

Court Reporter

Most depositions are memorialized using a court reporter. That means a person (the court reporter) will be seated near you at the deposition and will swear you in. She will typically use a laptop to record your testimony. Once the deposition is over, she will ask you if you want to "read and sign" the deposition. That is done to ensure accuracy. You will be required to go to her office to read the deposition.

If you request and pay for a transcript of the deposition, she will provide a certified transcript of your testimony. It can take weeks to receive. If you need it sooner than the regular turn-around time normally takes, you will be required to pay for expedited service.

It is important to know, most court reporters also audio record your testimony to ensure accuracy. If you take issue with the accuracy of the transcript, you may want to ask if you may listen to the recording. If the court reporter does not willingly turn over the recording, you may need to seek court intervention.

Video Deposition

Some depositions are memorialized by being video recorded and transcribed by a court reporter. You should be provided notice prior to the deposition if you are going to be video recorded. Check your local rules to ensure the rules have been followed.

If you are going to be video recorded you will want to ensure you are dressed and present yourself as if you were going to be in court.

My basic rules for dressing for the court include:

1. Be conservative. You want to appeal to the largest audience.
2. Cover tattoos
3. Remove all piercings, except one set of earrings for women.
4. Hair should be neatly combed/brushed. If you have long hair and tend to fiddle with it, pull it back.
5. Minimal make-up for women, no make-up for men.
6. No tight clothing or cleavage.
7. I tend to suggest light blue-, lavender-, white-, or cream-colored shirts. I suggest staying away from black or red or dark purple.

My basic rules are not meant to judge or put anyone down who dresses differently than I suggest or who has tattoos or piercings. My goal is help you appeal to the largest audience. A judge or juror may believe in negative stereotypes of tattooed people. You want to minimize that.

For video depositions you will also want to be aware of your body language. Keep your hands away from your face. If you are being accused of domestic violence or assault, don't sit in your chair with a puffed-up chest. Instead, bring your shoulders in and try to make yourself look a little smaller.

Unlike written transcription, anger shows up on video. Really, most emotions show up on video. You want to be sure to control your emotions. If you are being deposed for a divorce, this may be the first time you will have seen your ex in months or since the separation. You will likely be emotional. Plan for it. Use lavender on your temples to keep you calm. If you have time to exercise, meditate or do yoga before the deposition, do it.

Online Video Deposition

Although online video depositions were used prior to COVID, they were not nearly as prevalent as they are today. Even if you are on a video feed for your deposition, you likely are still required to have notice if the video deposition will be recorded. Check your local rules for clarification.

One bonus about an online deposition is that you can do the deposition from the comfort of your own home unless your attorney wants you in her office. But even if you are required to be in your attorney's office, you will be in a much more relaxed setting then if you are right next to a person in a large impersonal conference room.

Scope of Deposition

The attorney deposing you is permitted to ask you questions about anything that may possibly lead to admissible evidence. That means that they can ask you questions that would not be admissible in court. For instance, if you had an affair, that may not be admissible in court, however, it may lead to admissible evidence, i.e., marital waste.

Attorneys are usually not permitted to go on a fishing expedition and ask a bunch of irrelevant questions. However, sometimes it may seem as though attorneys do just that.

The judge in your case can limit the scope of the questioning at a deposition if there is a reasonable basis to do so. If you do want the judge to limit the scope you will need to have a really good reason. Talk to your lawyer if you want to limit the scope. But do so with the understanding that your lawyer is your advocate and knows what is best.

Limiting the Scope of Deposition

You may be able to ask the court to limit the scope of deposition. For instance, if you have trade secrets or a confidentiality agreement, you may want the court to order those issues to be off limits. To do that you will need to file a motion for a protective order prior to the deposition being taken.

If you attend the deposition without restrictions, and the attorney begins asking questions you do not believe should be answered, talk to your attorney. If you are unrepresented and adamant about not answering certain questions, you may need to call the judge.

In any case, if you choose not to answer a question, and your reason is not deemed reasonable, you may be sanctioned and required to reimburse the costs for that deposition. You may also be required to participate in another deposition. If you continue to refuse to answer the questions, you can be held in contempt.

Length/Time Limit of Deposition.

The length of deposition may vary between jurisdictions and even within a jurisdiction. Most jurisdictions will also permit a judge to modify the amount of time for the deposition.

For example, the Civil Federal Rules may permit a one (1) day, seven (7) hour deposition. However, state courts may permit four (4) hours for family court and six (6) hours for civil court. The time permitted will also depend on the complexity of the case. For instance, if you are in small claims court litigating over $5,000, there is probably no reason to have a seven-hour deposition. Alternatively, if you are in a wrongful death, medical malpractice, or a class action case, it might not be unusual for someone to be deposed for more than one day.

Review the rules and know the time limits so you or your attorney can require that the rules be followed.

It is also important to know that depositions often run long. Therefore, if there is a four-hour limit on a deposition, and an attorney has a good reason to extend it, the time should be extended. Each case is different. It might be reasonable to extend a deposition in a multi-million-dollar lawsuit. However, it may not be reasonable to extend a deposition in a small claims case.

One way to help ensure you are not stuck in the deposition for any more time than necessary is to answer the questions asked and not try to play games with the attorney conducting the deposition. It is not uncommon for a deponent to try to guess where the attorney is going and try not to give him the answer he wants. Don't try to guess. Just answer the question. In most cases, the attorney has been taking depositions for many years and can outsmart you. Just answer the question and move on.

What To Expect During Your Deposition

Knowing what to expect during your deposition will allow you to be more comfortable and relaxed during the deposition. When you are more relaxed you will have an easier time answering questions. While each attorney and each deposition are a little different, the basics are the same. You will be sworn in and you will be asked questions and your deposition will be memorialized by a court report and possibly a videographer.

What has changed significantly is that depositions are now often done over a video feed, such as Zoom. If you are high medical risk or have a fever or Covid, you should let your attorney know and/or the attorney who subpoenaed you. You will not want to spread Covid. Therefore, they may either permit you to appear via video or the attorney may reschedule the deposition all together.

In Person Deposition vs Video Deposition

Since Covid swept across the world, it is not unusual for depositions to be taken online via video feed. Typically, the attorney requesting the deposition decides whether the deposition will be taken in-person or online.

In-person depositions are, or at least before Covid were, the most frequently used types of deposition for most cases, with video depositions mostly being used when the deponent was in a different state or country. Many attorneys prefer in-person depositions because in-person depositions usually make the deponent a little less comfortable and the attorney can knock the deponent off kilter a bit more.

Since the outbreak of the Covid Pandemic, most law offices are pretty careful when it comes to stopping infected people from going into their offices. If you are feeling unwell, you should let your attorney or the deposing attorney know that you are not feeling well. If you are still able to testify for the deposition, they may change the deposition from in-person to online. If you are not able to testify because you are too sick, they will likely just reschedule.

An issue that occurs in family law depositions when doing in-person depositions is that your ex will very likely be in the room. If you are not comfortable seeing your ex, it can make the experience even worse than a deposition already is. You may need to do some relaxation techniques and focus on not looking at him/her.

What can also happen in an in-person deposition, is that other people may be permitted to attend if you have not filed for a protective order. I have only had someone attempt to do that one time. I was not required to file a protective order, because I told the attorney I would have the unagreed upon person escorted off the property for trespassing. Again, it rarely happens, but it can happen.

If you are testifying at an in-person deposition, you will be sitting at a table with several other people. (See table on next page.)

- The court reporter will likely be sitting at chair 1 or 5. They will need to have access to an electrical outlet. The typically have a laptop and will set that up at least 15 minutes ahead of time.

- You, the deponent, will sit closest to the court reporter. That means you should either sit at 2/4 or 6/8 (depending on what side your lawyer is on). This seating position is important to ensure the court reporter can hear you.

- Your attorney will sit next to you in seat 3 or 7.

- The opposing counsel will probably sit across from you and next to the court reporter. Again, this helps to ensure the court reporter will be able to clearly hear the questions being asked.

- The opposing party, if he/she attend will sit next to their attorney.

- Anyone else who attends the deposition will in the empty seat on the side of the table who they are there for.

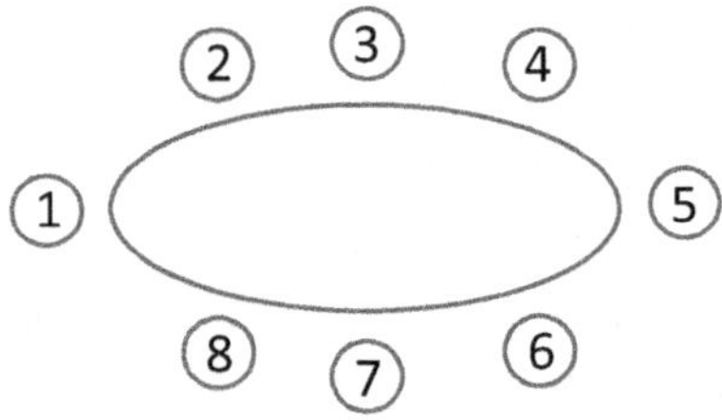

The table may be smaller or larger or a different shape. However, the seating arrangement and the reason for the seating arrangement will remain consistent.

Deposition When There Has Been Domestic Violence

If you have been a victim of domestic violence, being in the same room as your ex may be terrifying. You can ask to have safeguards put into place. If your ex is represented, you can ask that your ex not be permitted in the room. One way to do that is to have your ex on a video feed or on a speakerphone.

Depending on the severity of the domestic violence, you may need to get the court involved. If you have an order of protection, the judge may be more protective than if you just say you are a victim.

Procedure of The Deposition

1. Swearing in:

   You will be asked to stand and raise your right had to be sworn in. Depending on the jurisdiction, they may or may not add "So help me God." Once you agree in the affirmative, you will sit down (if you were standing) and you will begin the deposition.

2. Admonishment/Statement by Attorney

   The attorney questioning you will usually talk to you about rules of the deposition. They are typically as follows:

   - Please listen to the question and don't speak over the attorney. Please wait until the question is completed before answering.
     - This is done to ensure the court reporter can take an accurate record.
     - The court reporter can only type so fast and can only hear one person at a time without the real possibility of the court reporter making errors in the transcript.

   - If you do not understand the question, please ask her to repeat or rephrase the question or let her know you don't understand the question.
     - This is to ensure you are answering the right question.

- - o   If you misunderstand the question, you may be stuck with testimony that says something other that what you thought it said.

- You need to answer audibly, and do not answer with uh hu or mmhmm and no nodding your head.
  - o   Again, this is to ensure you have an accurate record of the testimony.

- You may be asked if you are on any drugs or alcohol that would preclude you from answering honestly.
  - o   Do not take offense to this. Most lawyers ask this question. They need to be sure that you don't later come back and say that you were on too much pain medication to know what was going on or that you drank too much.

- You will usually be told that you can ask to take a break when needed, but that any outstanding questions should be answered first.
  - o   You should take a break when you need to. Don't feel bad about that. You need to answer any outstanding question before leaving to assure the attorney you are not seeking outside coaching on how to answer. But take a break when you want.

Questions

You will be asked questions by the attorney who subpoenaed you. That attorney is seeking information that may help them better understand the case along with information they can use against you. Keep that in mind when answering questions.

After you are deposed, your attorney (or you if you are unrepresented) may be permitted to ask a couple questions to help clarify some of the answers. Attorneys do not always do this. The time when this would most frequently happen would be when you, or the witness, will not be available for trial and all the information, for both sides of the litigation, will need to be available for the judge to consider.

Attorney Objections

Most deponents will want their attorney to "protect" them from being harassed by the deposing attorney. Unfortunately, your attorney's hands are somewhat tied. Your attorney is permitted to object on "form" and/or "foundation". However, even if your attorney objects, you will still be required to answer the question unless you are advised not to by your attorney or you plead the 5th. Meaning that you are not going to incriminate yourself by answering the question.

An objection for "FORM" means that the questions was not asked correctly. For instance, sometimes an attorney will make a statement in such a way that is really not a question, but they want you to confirm it.

Example: And then you went to the doctor after being hit?

It's really not a question. It's a statement that you went to the doctor. If you understand the question, you can answer. If your attorney objects for "form" you may want to think about the question and ask the attorney to reword the question.

Your attorney may also object if there is a compound question. That means there are two separate questions in on sentence.

Example: Isn't it true that you took money out of your bank account and spent it on your girlfriend.

You may have taken money out of the account but you may not have spent it on your girlfriend. You cannot answer yes, because you don't know what you would be admitting to. You can't answer no because you did take money out. If something like this happens you should ask the deposing attorney to rephrase the question.

Your attorney may also object on the basis of "FOUNDATION". That means that part of the question presumes something that has not yet been testified to or you need more information to accurately answer the question.

Example: Isn't it true that you emailed her more than 20 times in one day.

You would want to know who "her" is and you would want to know a date. If your attorney objects for foundation, you may want to ask for the questions to be rephrased or if they could be more specific.

You don't want to come off sounding like a jerk, but you also do not want to answer a question inaccurately. Remember, you are giving testimony, and this testimony can be used against you.

There are exceptions that permit your attorney to objection based on just "form" and "foundation". These are not really exceptions to the objections but more like attorney involvement. Your attorney can advise you not to answer a question. That would be done if answering the question would require you to divulge a trade secret, attorney client privilege or any other type of protected information. Follow your attorney's lead. If you are representing yourself, be careful not to testify about any privileged information. This is especially important if it is not your privilege to waive.

You attorney may advise you not to answer a question if the answer would incriminate you in a crime. Your attorney may advise you not to answer if your answer would divulge privileged information. You attorney may advise you not to answer a question that is irrelevant, not likely to lead to admissible evidence and asked solely for the purpose of harassing you. However, it is very uncommon for attorneys to advise you to not answer on the basis of irrelevance or harassment.

Sometimes it may seem as though your attorney is not protecting you, and that may or may not be true. Your attorney may just want you to push through it to get it over with. If your attorney advises you to walk out of the deposition, you may incur significant attorney fees fixing what happened. For instance, your attorney might have to file a motion, which will cost you money, and may be required to have an oral argument in court, which will cost you money, and you may be required to attend another deposition with limitations, which will cost you more money. Your attorney likely wants to protect you very much. However, if you can handle being harassed for a little while, it may actually save you thousands of dollars. Is that fair? No, absolutely not. But it is reality.

Non- Expert Answering Questions

When answering questions there really is a right way and a wrong way. Sometimes it can take a lot of work for clients to learn how to actually answer the question correctly and to not speak too much about things other than simply answering the question.

When preparing clients for deposition I try to determine how they will testify by finding out if they are "over-explainers" and/or if they have any other communication habits that could cause them to provide the other side with information to use against them.

I often ask this question:

EXAMPLE:

You and I just finished having lunch on Shea and the 101 freeway, and you are driving to work afterwards. While driving to work you typically take the 101 Freeway to the 202 Freeway, then exit and on 44th street then you pull into your office parking lot. However, on your way today, you got on the 101 Freeway and there was an accident, so you got off on Chaparral and took that to Hayden Road. But there was a detour from Hayden, so you had to get off on Camelback. You then took Camelback to 44th Street and took 44th Street to work.

If I call you and ask where you are, what will you say?

1. I'm on Camelback and 44th Street? Or,
2. I was on the 101 and there was an accident so I got off on Chaparral and went to Hayden then there was a detour so you had to take Camelback to 44th Street?

This is an example that will help me, or really you, determine if you are an over-explainer. If you are an over-explainer, you will need to prepare a bit differently for your deposition, such as listening to the question and answering the question. When I prepare an over-explaining client, I strongly urge them to practice with family members for usually at least a week before the deposition. As you can see above, scenario #2, the person answering never actually answered the question of: Where are you?

Another example I use is this:

Can you tell me how old your kids are?

- If you say 4 and 6, you did not answer the question.
- If you say Yes, Billy is 4 and Julie is 6, you did answer the question and you continued speaking.
- If you answered – YES, you have correctly answered the question. Because the only question was . . . Can you tell me how old your kids are?

However, this is just an example to help you understand about answering questions and pointing out very common mistakes. This example shows how easy it can be to not listen to the question and not even really answer the question.

In a deposition and in trial, giving a child's name or age is not a big problem. However, minimizing the response and not giving more than asked should be the rule. Providing more information than what was asked for should be the exception. It is really important to pay attention to the question and answer the question.

You will often want to explain things or clarify things during a deposition. I think that comes naturally. Most of the time it is not necessary. However, there are exceptions. For example, if you were in an accident and you hurt your right shoulder in the accident, but five years ago you had surgery on your left shoulder. You may want to clarify if asked the following questions:

Q: Isn't it true you had surgery on your shoulder five years ago?

A: Yes, I had surgery on my left shoulder.

You added a little clarification and that was fine in this case. However, you want to keep clarifications at a minimum. Let the person deposing you ask the question and you answer the question asked. Again, providing *more* than the answer "yes" is the exception, not the rule.

In deposition, you will often be asked open ended questions. You will be asked "why" or "how" and you will need to provide more than one- or two-word answers. In this case, you will want to try to limit your sentences. Try to keep your answers between one and five sentences if possible. And really be thoughtful before answering. If you are an expert being deposed, you may need to provide longer answers to thoroughly explain you findings and the reasoning behind your findings.

It is important to remember that you are not just telling your story, but you are *testifying* about your story. Testifying about your story is more formal and should be taken more seriously than how you would tell your story to a friend. You need to tell your story with more precision and less embellishment.

It is also really important to tell the truth. You can tell the truth without saying everything. For instance, a person who had companies in more than one state was concerned that it would be used against her. She was also very sure she would be asked about it. So how do you minimize a question when someone is trying to paint you in a bad light? Her main business was in Washington, but she lived in Arizona and her family was in Arizona and during the marriage she traveled regularly. But she wanted to minimize the fact that her business was so far away. After some discussion, we decided this is how she would answer the question.

Example:

Q: Isn't it true you have a business in Washington?

A: Yes, and also in Arizona.

But she didn't need to answer the question like that. She could have simply said, "yes". Her attorney later would have the opportunity to clarify it, either in the deposition, through correspondence through counsel or through testifying in court.

The rule of thumb is, if you are asked a yes or no question, you should answer yes or no. But there are exceptions and if they are well thought out, they should be okay. The problem comes in when they are not well thought out and/or when they are blurted out without thought, often due to emotion – anger and frustration generally.

Another trick lawyers like to use is to leave you in silence after you thought you were finished answering the question. They may stare at you until you say something else or even fidget with their papers in the silence. Many people are uncomfortable with silence. I always recommend deponents become comfortable with silence and simply enjoy the time between questions. You should not try to fill the gap of silence by speaking. If you have answered the question, leave it at that.

Do NOT guess at an answer. If you do not know an answer, simply say you do not know the answer. Do not try to come up with an answer if you do not know it. The attorney may try to narrow a time frame down by asking you if you know what year or what season something happened. If you know, you can answer. If you do not know and you are not able to remember based on the attorney's prodding, do not answer. But if you are able to be reminded, feel free to answer.

Example:

Q:		When is the last time you saw the defendant?

A:		I don't know. It's been a few years for sure.

Q:		Do you know if it was within the last two years?

A:		I don't know, I don't want to guess.

Q:		Could it have been 10 years ago?

A:		No, I didn't even know him 10 years ago.

Q:		So sometime between 10 years ago and today?

(Objection, form . . . this is one of those non questions)

A: I'm sorry, can you rephrase the question?

Q: Would you agree that the last time you saw him was sometime between 10 years ago, and today?

A: Yes.

Q: When did you meet him?

A: About 8 years ago.

Q: Where did you meet him?

A: At U Mass Boston.

Q: Did you see him often during the time you attended UMass?

(Objection, Foundation. No one said you actually attended UMASS – but if you did, just answer the question.)

A: Yes.

Q: Did you see him at all after you graduated?

(Objection, Foundation. You have not testified yet that you graduated from UMASS, and he did not specifically say graduating from UMASS. So, if you attended another school later that could be a problem. You may just want to ask for clarification or clarify yourself.)

A: Yes.

Q: What was your relationship?

A: We dated after we graduated.

Q: For how long did you date?

A: About a year or so.

Q: When did you break up?

A: About 5 years ago.

Q: Have you seen him since you broke up?

A: Yes.

Q: Under what circumstances did you see him?

A: I've run in to him here and there.

Q: Did you ever purposefully meet up with him after you broke up?

A: I don't recall. (If you don't remember that is totally fine. You are not required to remember everything.)

Q: Is there anything that could help you call?

A: I suppose if you told me a specific time that you think I may have done that it might jog my memory. But I don't have any independent recollection at this time.

Q: Ok. Thank you. What about the little bar on Central and Portland Avenue about three years ago?

A: I didn't purposefully meet him there. He followed me there and sat down at my table. And I am unsure how long ago that was.

Q: Well, if I told you he believes it was about 3 years ago, would you have any reason to doubt me?

A: I would actually have no reason to believe his memory. He's not very honest. **_OR_** Since I'm testifying under oath, I'd prefer only to testify about things I personally remember.

Q: Have you seen him since that time?

A: No.

Q:	Do you recall where you lived when you saw him?

A:	Yes, I lived down town?

Q:	And do you still live there?

A:	No.

Q:	How long has it been since you lived there?

A:	About two years.

Q:	So, you definitely haven't seen him in the last two years, is that fair to say?

A:	Yes.

So, the attorney may be able to jog your memory somewhat, just by asking questions that you can mentally put in a timeline. Don't be afraid to take the trip down memory lane with the attorney. Just be sure to not agree to anything you do not know for sure.

You might have been able to talk yourself through this all by yourself had he not jogged your memory. But if you do that, it should not be out loud – and it's not your job.

It is also really important not to admit to something if you do not have factual knowledge that it is the truth. Sometimes attorneys will say something like, would you have any reason not to trust me if I said there was $5,000 in the account on May 1st? This happens all too often and the response is typically something like, "If you say so." However, it would be better if the exchange looked something like this:

EXAMPLE:

Q:	Are you aware of the amount of money in that account on May 1st?

A:	No.

Q: Well, if I told you there was $5,000 in the account would you have any reason to not believe me?

A: Since I am providing sworn testimony, I'd prefer not to testify to something I don't have first-hand knowledge of.

The deposition is being taken to memorialize YOUR testimony, not the lawyer's testimony. You will be held responsible for what you say in the deposition. You need to be sure you can stand by it.

Outstanding Discovery Requests

You may be asked to provide certain documents or recordings or other evidence or property to the questioning attorney. Don't simply agree to be agreeable. You should probably have a formal request so you don't forget about it and it should go through your attorney if you have one.

EXAMPLE:
Q: I sent you a request for documents and things, do you recall that?

A: Yes.

Q: Did you provide everything I asked for?

A: I think I did.

Q: Okay, thank you for that. There are some outstanding items. We asked for recordings are you aware of that?

A: I honestly don't recall. (Don't say honestly. You have sworn to tell the truth, so saying honestly is redundant and causes ears to perk up.)

Q: When you recorded your ex, did you do so on your phone?

A: Usually, yes.

Q: Did you bring that cell phone here with you today? (It's just better not to bring your cell phone with you if there is anything on it that is private.)

A: Yes

Q: Can you forward me the recordings now? (Objection, are you asking my client to have private communication with you?)

A: I'd prefer everything go through my attorney.

Q: I apologize. Can you send it to your attorney as we sit here?

A: I'd prefer to talk to my attorney prior to sending anything from my phone. (It's okay to defer to your attorney.)

•

Being Misquoted

Lawyers may misquote you about something you said. Don't give in to that. It's okay to say you did not say that.

EXAMPLE:

Q: Did you see Brittany at a club?

A: Yes

Q: Did you dance with her?

A: Yes

Q: Did you buy her a drink?

A: Yes

. . . . . Several questions asked that have nothing to do with the Brittany.

Q: Sorry, I wanted to get back to your relationship with Brittany. When did you start dating?

A: We didn't

Q: Well didn't you say you went clubbing with her and bought her drinks?

A: No, that's not what I said.

Be sure not to let the attorney put words in your mouth. If they do, you are stuck with that answer.

Do not joke or answer facetiously. It does not look good when transcribed.

I had a friend once that answered: Oh yeah, right! Jokingly, and it came out as if she agreed with the question. She did not. It was the exact opposite of agreeing.

Sometimes you will be asked a question that includes language that is subjective. Words like – many, large, big, several, a lot, and minimal, along with many other words, are quite subjective and can have a different meaning to you than to someone else. Try to stay away from answering questions that have these types of words without asking for some clarity.

EXAMPLE:

Q: Isn't it true that you only helped minimally?

A: I'm sorry, I don't know what you mean by "minimally".

Q: Well, did you help a lot or a little?

A: Again, I'm sorry, I'm not sure what you mean by a lot or a little. Could you maybe give me a timeframe or something?

Q:	Well, how about you give me a timeframe for the amount of time you helped work.

A:	I probably helped for three hours.

Q:	And do you know how long it actually took to complete the job?

A:	No. (If you know the answer, fine. If you do not, don't guess.)

Exhibits During Deposition

You may also be shown some exhibits during your deposition. The attorney will provide a copy to the court reporter to "mark". That means the court reporter will put a sticker on the exhibit and assign it a number. The first exhibit will be marked with a "1" and so on.

You will then be provided the copy of the exhibit to testify about. Your attorney should also be provided a copy and will likely mark it with the assigned number.

If you are asked a specific question about the exhibit, make sure you answer only about what you know about. This is another situation where an attorney might try to demand that you simply agree with him. However, you are not required to and in fact you should not simply acquiesce because the attorney is being forceful.

EXAMPLE:

Q: Isn't it true that you took $3,000 out of the bank account on August 6, 2021?

A: I don't recall, can you show me where that is in these documents?

Q: It's on the page marked August 6, 2021.

A: Okay, I'm sorry, there are hundreds of pages so it may take me a minute for me to find it.

Q: Well I'm telling you, you took $3,000 out on August 6, 2021, do you have any reason not to believe me?

A: I'd just prefer to verify since I am testifying under oath.

You have every right, and even the responsibility to be sure that your testimony is accurate. You should not provide any testimony that you do not have first hand knowledge of.

It is also important to tell the truth. You will be held to whatever you testify to. If you testify that you removed $3,000 from the account, you are stuck with that answer and you may need to explain it to the court. In reality, maybe you did not remove the $3,000. Maybe it was an error. Maybe your ex removed the $3,000. Maybe you removed it and put it right back in. Maybe you removed it on another day. You may not get the opportunity to explain that if you agree to something that you don't know.

DOs and DON'Ts When Answering Questions

- Do not guess
  - Remember, you are testifying under oath. If you say you spent over $15,000 on medical expenses, be sure you spent over $15,000 on medical expenses. You will be stuck with that amount. If you really spent $13,000, you now have provided testimony that can be used against you. There are often ways to correct this information, but sometimes, if your deposition is being used, and you are not testifying, it may not get corrected.
- Do not estimate unless your estimate if fairly precise and you are certain of your numbers.
  - Between 6 and 8 hours. If you are not 100% sure it is between 6 and 8 hours, do not say it is.
- Do not get angry
  - I know this is easier said than done. But it is so important. An angry witness is one of the easiest witnesses to get information from. Angry witnesses also seem to need to explain why they are right. When an angry witness starts explaining, she will usually give too much testimony.
  - Do what you need to do to not get angry. I always recommend putting lavender on your temples, exercise, deep breathing, meditation or prayer.
- Do not ask a question back.
  - This often happens when a deponent gets emotional. "Well, what would you do if you caught your wife in bed with your best friend?"

- Do not act snotty.
  - Tone can be detected in person and in the depositions that are recorded by video. Although you cannot necessarily detect tone in a written transcript, a snotty tone never helps in a deposition.
- Do not get into an argument with the attorney.
  - If an attorney is trying to push you into an answer with which you don't agree, just say, you don't agree. Don't argue. Just state your answer. If asked why, state your reasoning.
- Do not talk yourself through an answer out loud.
  - When you talk yourself through to get to an answer, everything will be on record. If you misremember or forget something you will be held to that answer. If you want to ask to think about it for a minute, that is fine. But if you don't know or don't remember, just say that.
- Don't yell or clinch your fists.
  - Even if there is no camera, the other attorney may put your physical appearance on the record. So, keep that in mind. I have on more than one occasion described what was happening in the court room.
    - *For the record, Mr. Smith just looked at Ms. Smith and smirked at her when I asked that question.*
  - I would then follow up with questions. Why did you smirk at Ms. Smith?
- Do act professionally.
- Do take breaks when needed.
- Do pay attention to your attorney.
- Do pause before answering a question.
- Do be sure to answer the question.

- Do be on time for your deposition.
- Do practice answering questions appropriately.
- Do examine exhibits before answering any questions about them.
- Do not be bullied into answering a question a certain way.
- Do not be bullied into guessing.

Expert Deposition Preparation

I believe it is important to be honest during your deposition. When exerts prepare reports, they provide a lot of evidence that may, at times, be used against them.

As an expert, when you testify in a deposition every word of your testimony will be critiqued. It is important to understand that. Attorneys may look through your notes, psychological test results, Curriculum Vitae, website, past reports, documents and recordings provided by the parties, police, and doctors so they can pick apart your report/opinion. If one party does not like your report, they will most certainly try to minimize its validity or worse prove the entire report is invalid. Your testimony will be key to maintaining or ensuring the persuasiveness of your report/opinion.

It is also important to set a goal and keep that goal in mind when you are answering questions. Do you want to make sure you validate your report, even if it is wrong or misrepresents the facts? Or do you want to be accurate and give a deposition based on honesty, even if that means owning your mistakes? As much as you might want to validate your report and also give accurate testimony, those may be mutually exclusive. It is important to know this goal before testifying in a deposition and in court. If you do not have this goal at the forefront of your mind, you may start talking in circles by agreeing that you made errors and that they are significant, but then not changing your recommendation. In that case your testimony may seem to contradict itself.

You must also remember, after the deposition, the attorneys will have an opportunity to pick apart everything in your deposition and cross examine you again in court on the witness stand in front of the judge. They may also have another expert testifying about alleged errors in your report. If there are significant errors, you may want to address them sooner rather than later and possibly even provide an amended report.

I've most frequently seen fixable errors in forensic accounting reports and business valuations. If the expert had an adding error or considered one issue but not another, it may create a significant difference. If it is addressed right away, the admission of the error really almost validates the rest of your report.

If you are going to validate your report no matter what, then you are going to need to be aware of the shortfalls in the report and figure out how to show those issues would not affect the outcome of your report.

EXAMPLE:

Notes taken during Child Interview: Father made children dinner every night and sometimes they helped.

Report: Father did not make children dinner.

Was this a typo or is this issue important enough to have changed the outcome of your recommendations? To validate your report, it seems it must be either a typo or it is not important enough to change the outcome. However, if you think this is really significant and you need to change your report or you would update the recommendations based on your new information, you need to admit that and admit that you made an error.

As soon as you know you are going to be deposed, I strongly urge you to review your report. You should also take some time to review your notes and other information you considered when creating your report. If you find any discrepancies, you will need to determine how to explain those away. Or, you will need to make corrections. Either way, and no matter what you choose, you should make that decision prior to attending the deposition. You should have a direction to follow.

The information provided above in the "Non-Expert" section is also applicable to you as an expert; and it should be read in conjunction with this section. However, experts do require additional preparation because they may be held to a higher standard in court. Experts are not fact witnesses; therefore everything from their education to the biases can come in to question. If you are a paid expert by one party, the court might believe you are less credible than an expert that was appointed by the court. Because your credibility is so important, you must be able to back up your testimony with facts that correspond with your findings/opinions.

Be prepared to talk about your education and post degree continuing education. If you have written any articles or you have been published in professional journals, be sure to mention that if possible. If there is a certain issue in the case, such as domestic violence, review what training you have taken on domestic violence. As stated above, if the case involves domestic violence and you are a psychologist testifying regarding the party's mental health; you may want to inform the court of all the domestic violence training you have taken.

Don't let an attorney button-hole you into answering their question in a way that you don't believe is appropriate.

EXAMPLE:

Q:	Isn't it true you did an evaluation in this case?

A:	Yes

Q:	And it looks like you found that Father committed significant domestic violence, correct?

A:	Correct.

Q: How did you come up that finding?

A: I evaluated the evidence, and weighed the facts against the statute requirements.

Q: When you say you weighed the facts, what facts did you use?

A: Well, I took Mother's responses and Father's responses and outside evidence, and I determined there was significant domestic violence.

Q: So, did you give each bit of evidence equal weight?

A: No. I think I gave more weight to Mother's testimony than to Father's because her stories were more consistent?

Q: Okay, so was it Mother 60% and Father 40%?

A: I can't really quantify it.

Q: Well, if you had to quantify, what would you quantify it as?

A: I'm sorry, it's not something that can be quantified. (Stick to your answer and don't get bullied into making something up.)

Q: So, are you saying you won't quantify or you can't.

A: Both.

It's important to not be pressured by an attorney into doing or saying something that just does not make sense to you. Experts typically review a lot of information which allows them to provide an expert opinion. Just let the questioning attorney know how you arrived at your opinion.

An attorney may also try to get you to change your opinion or recommendation and there may be a situation where it would be appropriate to change your opinion. For instance, if the facts are very specific, but you were not aware of some of those facts, an attorney might ask whether knowing those facts might change your opinion? The answer may be yes. You did not have those facts for your report, so it does not diminish your credibility.

Representing Yourself for Your Deposition

If you have received a subpoena requiring you to be deposed and you are not represented by an attorney, you will be your own representative. You may not need representation depending on your role in a case. For instance, if you are a fact witness (maybe you witnessed a car accident) then you will just go tell the attorney what you saw.

Even when you are a fact witness, one attorney may still want to trip you up. This is not uncommon and you shouldn't really take it personally. You may be asked questions about medications, about your vision, about your memory, whether anyone is paying you . . . anything really to try and make you look bad.

If you represent yourself, you may want to preserve your record with objections. It might be helpful to research "form" and "foundation" objections. It is also really important to not only know the rules, but you should also print them out and take them with you. Know them and have them available. However, you if you feel like you need to "object" you can also just ask for clarification instead.

EXAMPLE:

Q: Did you witness a car accident?

A: Can you please be more specific? (You may have witnessed 10 car accidents. You want to be sure you are speaking about the same thing the attorney is thinking about.)

Q: Did you witness a car accident on September 3, 2021?

A: Yes.

EXAMPLE:

Q: Did you go to the mall after you saw Jill with the baby?

A: That's two questions. So, I did see Jill with the baby, but I went to a grocery store, not the mall. (Or you can ask the attorney to rephrase the question.)

It's important to be sure you answer the questions in a way that accurately reflects the truth. If you just said yes, you would have admitted to seeing Jill and going to the mall.

If, after you are done being deposed, you believe that something was not explained or clarified, you should make a note to do so at the end. With the understanding that in most cases you should speak as little as possible.

After the Deposition

After the deposition you will be asked if you would like to "read and sign". That likely means that you will be required to go to the court reporter's office and read the entire deposition and sign it. I recommend doing so. If you are unable to do so, review the deposition as soon as you have it to ensure the correctness. If there are errors, speak to your attorney immediately.

Attorneys will often try to reach settlement agreements after depositions. Depositions can help attorneys and parties determine the strengths and weaknesses of their cases, which can help during negotiations. A deposition can also show the attorneys if you are a good or bad witness. If you appear to be unreliable and cannot answer an easy question, the other side may choose to go to trial. Your deposition is important for many reasons, not just providing answers.

I do suggest you review the deposition prior to attending trial, if you do attend trial. Reviewing the deposition can help remind you what the attorney was focusing on. For instance, if the attorney continues to ask you questions about how certain money was spent from a joint bank account, you will know that is an area where they are likely planning to go after you.

How The Deposition Will Be Used

Depositions are used in many ways.

1. The most common reason for a deposition is to gather information. However, depositions can be used for more than just gathering information.
2. A deposition may also be used for settlement purposes.
    - They are useful for settlement purposes because attorneys can often get a better handle on what exactly someone wants. For instance, in a civil suit between neighbors, maybe one neighbor just wants an apology and an admission that the other party was wrong.
    - They can be used for settlement because the attorneys will be able to assess the credibility of the witness and determine how he will do in trial.
3. A deposition may be used in trial for cross examination.
    - The deposition may be used to cross examine the deponent and or to focus the testimony. Remember, attorneys will often have more time to depose someone then they will have to cross examine that person in trial. So, the deposition can help them focus on what is important.
4. The deposition can also be used in trial instead of the witness appearing in person. It may be read aloud in trial without the deponent even present.

When a deposition is used for trial, the party using the deposition may be required to designate sections of the deposition that will be used for trial. That means the party using the deposition will need to provide the page number and line number of sentence or sentences they wish to use in trial. Check your local rules.

General Deposition Preparation and Reminders

1. Do what you can to get relaxed before the deposition. If you have time to run or exercise, I recommend you do so. I also recommend using lavender on your temples.
2. Do be on time. Running late can cause anxiety. You don't want to be anxious when you testify during a deposition.
3. Do make sure you answer the question asked, not the question you *think* you were asked.
4. Do try to keep your answers between one and three sentences.
5. Do not offer to provide discovery to the questioning attorney without an okay from your attorney.
6. Do not joke or be factitious.
7. Remember that you are giving sworn testimony. Be truthful.
8. Do not try to guess what the questioning attorney is trying to get you to say. Just answer the question honestly.

Good luck with your deposition. I hope this book helped to provide information that was or will be useful during your deposition.

Check out our other books.

- Custody Evaluation Preparation
- Controlling Your Divorce & Building Your Case